OUT OF THIS WORLD

CAN YOU SEE WHAT I SEE?

OUT OF THIS WORLD

by Walter Wick

CARTWHEEL BOOKS

An Imprint of Scholastic Inc.

CARTWHEEL BOOKS

Published by Scholastic Inc.

SCHOLASTIC, CARTWHEEL BOOKS,

and associated logos are trademarks and/or

registered trademarks of Scholastic Inc.

TO NOAH AND EMMETT PARK

ISBN 978-0-545-24468-8

10 9 8 7 6 5 4 3 2 1   13 14 15 16 17 18/0

Printed in Singapore   46

First printing, January 2013

Book Design by Walter Wick and David Saylor

Library of Congress Cataloging-in-Publication Data

Wick, Walter, 1953-

Can you see what I see? : out of this world / by Walter Wick.   p. cm.

ISBN 978-0-545-24468-8

1. Picture puzzles--Juvenile literature. I. Title.

GV1507.P47W51345 2013

793.73--dc23   2012003523

CONTENTS

Can you see
what I see?
A fountain, 5 horses,
a fox, a goose,
a chipmunk, a sheep,
a dog, a moose,
a pumpkin, a carriage,
a rooster, a hen,
a spool, 2 swords,
a bull in a pen,
an apple, 3 hearts,
a high-flying crow,
and a princess castle
from long, long ago.

Can you see
what I see?
Falling water,
2 trumpets, a bell,
a flying horse,
3 swans, a shell,
4 wise owls,
a long red gown,
a moon, 3 dragons,
a peacock crown,
a key to a heart,
a hare on the run,
and a princess rising
with the morning sun!

Can you see
what I see?
A bow and arrow,
6 birds, a bat,
3 elephants,
a spotted cat,
a butterfly,
3 bees, a key,
a unicorn,
a tapestry,
a leaping deer,
a drowsy sheep,
and a castle guard
who's fast asleep!

Can you see
what I see?
Aladdin's lamp,
a frog, a lizard,
3 arrows, a flag,
a wise old wizard,
a skull, 3 candles,
a scorpion tail,
a bridge, a boat,
a turtle, a whale,
3 camels, a crab,
8 birds in all,
and the princess
at her crystal ball!

Can you see
what I see?
A magic wand,
a black cat, a crow,
3 dragonflies,
5 hearts in a row,
a lightning bolt,
a skeleton key,
a golden feather,
3 rabbits, a bee,
5 suns, a serpent,
a moon that's blue,
and a wide-eyed robot
staring back at you!

Can you see
what I see?
A mouse, a magnet,
a crescent moon,
a signal tower,
a silver spoon,
a wrench, a racket,
a rubber band,
a guitar gauge,
a minute hand,
2 springs, 3 wings,
a pen, a book,
and a robot with
a worried look!

Can you see
what I see?
4 marble planets,
a swan, a hare,
a lizard, a snake,
an aquatic pair,
a crane, a crab,
an archer, a scale,
a dragon, a unicorn,
a scorpion's tail,
3 silver jacks,
celestial lace,
and the Time Traveler
lost in space.

Can you see
what I see?
A globe, an apple,
a top to spin,
stitches, a straw,
a red clothespin,
a fan, 5 robots,
a windup key,
a crayon, a crown,
a bumblebee,
a duck, 3 trucks,
an ice-cream cone,
and an X marking
the landing zone.

Can you see
what I see?
A lightning bolt,
the number 9,
a hammer, a bell,
a DANGER sign,
a moon, 3 stars,
a planet, a spring,
a thimble, a knight,
a crown for a king,
5 bowling pins,
a baseball, a broom,
and a spaceship landing
with a crash, bang, boom!

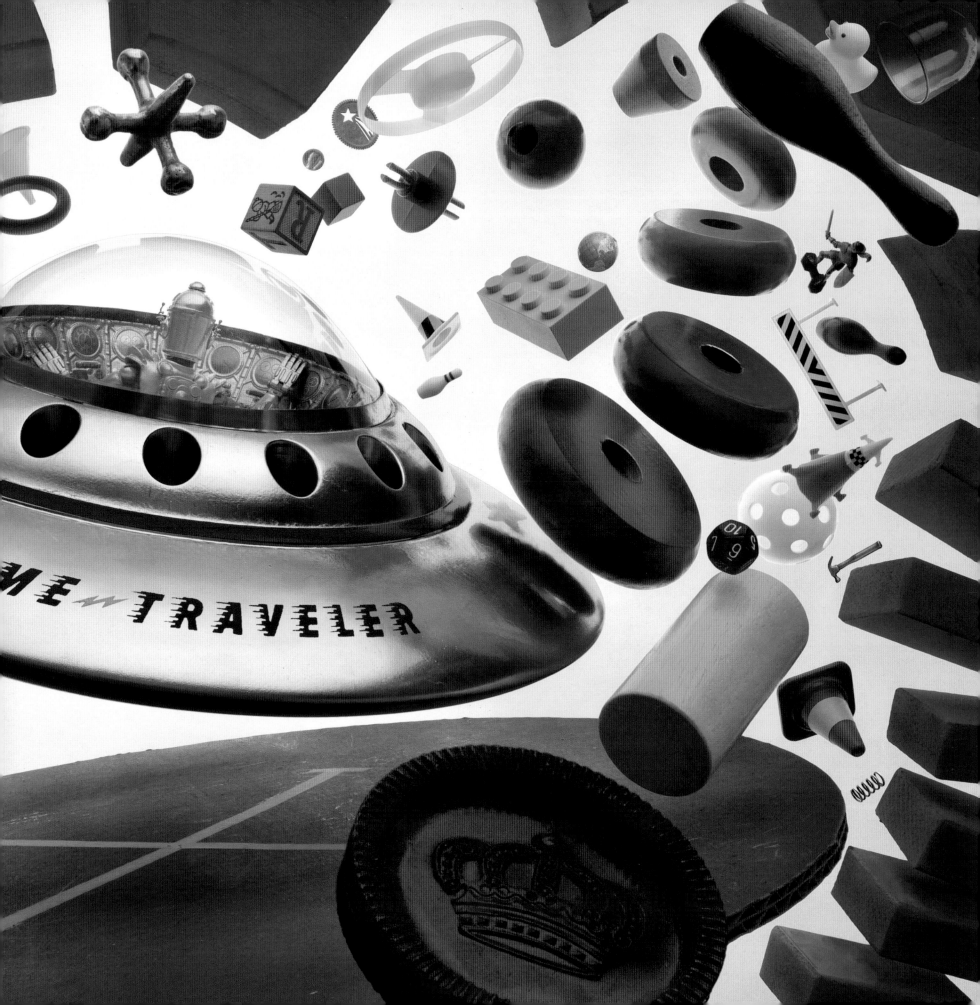

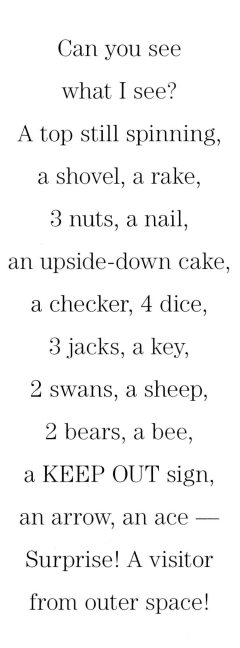

Can you see
what I see?
A top still spinning,
a shovel, a rake,
3 nuts, a nail,
an upside-down cake,
a checker, 4 dice,
3 jacks, a key,
2 swans, a sheep,
2 bears, a bee,
a KEEP OUT sign,
an arrow, an ace —
Surprise! A visitor
from outer space!

Can you see
what I see?
5 red diamonds,
a goblet, 4 fish,
a horse-drawn wagon,
a blueberry dish,
a sleepy dog,
2 cats, a hare,
a waterfall,
a lizard, a bear,
2 hilltop castles,
6 birds, a nest,
and a celebration
for a special guest.

Can you see
what I see?
A garden rebuilt,
a carriage, a clock,
3 dinosaurs,
a missing red sock,
a birdie, 5 rackets,
a bunny, 2 ducks,
3 baseballs, 3 bats,
a train, 4 trucks,
a Time Traveler
ready for flight —
Now it's time for all
to say good night!

Over the course of a year, my studio can resemble a kindergarten classroom run amok, the floor strewn with bins and boxes whose once orderly contents spill out on every available table and countertop. Amid one such moment, I found a plastic princess on my desk, staring frightfully at a wide-eyed tin robot that was standing next to her.

So it is that a princess and a robot meet in *Can You See What I See?: Out of This World*, the ninth title in the series. Putting these two unlikely characters together in a picture book had its challenges. Princesses recall the past; robots evoke the future. Princesses are soft and human; robots are hard-edged and mechanical. But as the details of the story emerged, I found similarities, too. The princess can see the future in her crystal ball; the robot can go back in time in his spaceship. The princess studies the stars on her astrological chart; the robot travels among the stars while using them for guidance. Ultimately, as the last scene reveals, these seemingly different worlds are really one and the same. For here, in an ordinary playroom with ordinary toys, when boys or girls are deeply immersed in creative play, any world is possible.

Acknowledgments

While my initial inspiration came from a store-bought princess and robot, a talented team of freelance artists and staff members made a custom princess and robot and numerous other props especially for this book. I would like to thank the team for their extraordinary contributions: to Randy Gilman for the construction of the "Time Traveler" robot, spaceship, cockpit interior, many pieces of custom furniture, the seated court figures, and countless other details small and large; to Michael Lokensgaard for building the princess, sleeping guard, and jesters, and for the scenic and faux painting throughout the castle interiors; to Drew Mailhot for his multitasking talent in both the workshop and the studio; to Lynne Steincamp for making the princess wig, clothing, and bedding; to Brian Keely-Dubois, who made computer models for 3-D printing of the 6-inch robot, the princess castle exterior, and several castle interior details. I would also like to thank studio manager Dan Helt for his expert overseeing of the workshop, studio, and computer operations; assistant Emily Cappa for her tireless prop management, hand-crafted miniature food in "Entertaining the Guest," and her valuable assistance with the rhymes; and my wife, Linda Cheverton Wick, for keeping all the behind-the-scenes operations running smoothly, for her expert artistic advice, and most of all, for her loving support.

I'd like to extend a heartfelt thanks to everyone at Scholastic who helped me make the Can You See What I See? series the best that it can be. I would especially like to thank editor Ken Geist and creative director David Saylor for their wise advice, designer Deena Fleming for her cover design, marketing director Julie Amitie for her tireless support, and president Ellie Berger for continuing to believe.

—Walter Wick

All sets were designed, arranged, photographed, and digitally processed by the author. Spot illustrations were arranged by Randy Gilman and photographed by the author.

Walter Wick is the photographer of the I Spy series of books, with more than forty-three million copies in print. He is author and photographer of *A Drop of Water: A Book of Science and Wonder*, which won the Boston Globe/Horn Book Award for Nonfiction, was named a Notable Children's Book by the American Library Association, and was selected as an Orbis Pictus Honor Book and a CBC/NSTA Outstanding Science Trade Book for Children. *Walter Wick's Optical Tricks*, a book of photographic illusions, was named a Best Illustrated Children's Book by the *New York Times Book Review*, was recognized as a Notable Children's Book by the American Library Association, and received many awards, including a Platinum Award from the Oppenheim Toy Portfolio, a Young Readers Award from *Scientific American*, a *Bulletin* Blue Ribbon, and a Parents' Choice Silver Honor.

Can You See What I See?, published in 2003, appeared on the *New York Times* Bestseller List for twenty-two weeks. His most recent books in the bestselling Can You See What I See? series are *Dream Machine*, *Cool Collections*, *The Night Before Christmas*, *Once Upon a Time*, *On a Scary Scary Night*, *Treasure Ship*, and *Toyland Express*. Mr. Wick has invented photographic games for *GAMES* magazine and photographed covers for books and magazines, including *Newsweek*, *Discover*, and *Psychology Today*. A graduate of Paier College of Art, Mr. Wick lives in Connecticut with his wife, Linda.

More information about Walter Wick is available at
www.walterwick.com
and
www.scholastic.com/canyouseewhatisee/

TIME TRAVELER